THE PLANES THE ALLIES FLEW
IN WORLD WAR II

The Planes the Allies Flew
in World War II

BY DAVID C. COOKE

Dodd, Mead & Company · New York

PICTURE CREDITS

Library of Congress Catalog Card Number: 71-80711

Printed in the United States of America

FOREWORD

During much of the period from the end of World War I in 1918 to the beginning of World War II in 1939 the airplane as a military weapon was almost stagnant in development. Commercial aviation had forged ahead so rapidly that while the military still used planes which were similar to World War I designs in concept, commercial machines were not only faster and designed on more modern principles but were also far more dependable.

A change finally came over military aviation in the last four or five years before hostilities again broke out between the major nations of Europe. In the Allied countries, Great Britain led the way. Meanwhile, the military in the United States proceeded cautiously. The country was still bogged down in a great depression, and there was little money or need for machines of war, and even less for research.

When German troops smashed through Belgium and Holland and defeated France, much of this success could be credited to the bombers and fighters of Adolf Hitler's *Luftwaffe*. And suddenly the airplane achieved a prominence it had not enjoyed since the closing days of World War I. Old lessons were remembered, and in the United States the military beseeched designers to come up with airplanes capable of performance which even a few years previously would have been considered impossible.

As always, men of vision were ready to accept the challenge, and some of the aircraft they produced became true classics. In the space of those few hectic years, the aviation industry performed miracles of design and production.

Scores of different types of airplanes were involved in the aerial fighting of World War II, and many of these became household names to people who previously had held only little interest in aviation. The most famous of these airplanes which served on the Allied side are described and illustrated on the following pages in the approximate order of their appearance.

I lived through this dramatic period as an aviation writer and magazine editor. As a war correspondent, I had an opportunity to observe virtually all the airplanes described and pictured in this book, and I also flew in many of them. One of my greatest thrills, in fact, was flying in a Republic P-47 Thunderbolt single-seater—with the pilot sitting in my lap! Likewise I shall never forget the flights I had over Occupied France in Consolidated B-24 Liberators, Martin B-26 Marauders, and in a Lockheed P-38 Lightning that had been modified to carry a two-man crew.

This book, then, is a result of personal experience as well as careful research. I trust that the reader will find it both useful and interesting.

DAVID C. COOKE

For James and John Cooke—
my favorite nephews

CONTENTS

CONSOLIDATED PBY CATALINA

The Catalina was the most dependable seaplane in service with the U.S. Navy during the war. It was slow and awkward, yet it was a reliable workhorse and could undertake virtually any mission.

The PBY owed its basic design to the Consolidated P2Y sesquiplane flying boat, which was put into production in 1931. The following year the Navy asked for bids on a new flying boat with a range of at least 3,000 miles and a maximum speed of not less than 150 miles per hour. Consolidated won the competition with its XP3Y-1, which was later designated PBY-1. The original test model

established a new world's seaplane record on October 15, 1935, when it flew 3,281 miles nonstop.

In 1938, Consolidated produced an amphibian version of the Catalina. This was called the PBY-5A, and its ability to operate either from land or water improved the plane's versatility.

Catalinas comprised the Navy's main aerial striking force when the United States became involved in the war. The "Cats" were used for long-range patrol, for bombing, and for torpedo attacks against enemy surface vessels. One Catalina pilot was credited with sinking 20 Japanese ships.

When production finally came to an end in March, 1945, a total of 3,074 Catalinas had been

Amphibian version of the sturdy Catalina was called PBY-5A. The first of these was completed in 1938.

Inside a gun blister on a Catalina. Note belt feed and sight for the .50-caliber swivel machine gun.

A PBY-5A making a full-stall landing. The plane was slow, but it could undertake virtually any mission.

built—2,398 by Consolidated and 676 by other companies.

Other data (PBY-5): Wing span, 104 feet; length, 65 feet 2 inches; loaded weight, 27,080 pounds; engines, two 1,200-horsepower Pratt & Whitney Twin Wasps; maximum speed, 190 miles per hour at 10,500 feet.

The PBY-6A was the final production Catalina. It had better armament and range than earlier models.

BOEING B-17 FLYING FORTRESS

On August 8, 1934, the Boeing Airplane Company received an announcement from the U.S. Army Air Corps that a design competition would be held for a new multiengined bomber. According to the specifications, the plane would be required to carry a bomb load of 2,000 pounds not less than 1,020 miles at a speed of at least 200 miles per hour. The announcement also specified that a flying test model would have to be ready no later than August, 1935.

Boeing immediately went to work on the project. But while other manufacturers took "multiengined" to mean two engines, Boeing decided to use four engines in its design. The experimental model of the new airplane, the Model 299, was taken up for its first flight on July 28, 1935.

The Boeing design was the largest landplane in the United States, and the world's fastest bomber. The test model far exceeded the required specifica-

tions. It had a range of 3,010 miles, a carrying capacity of 4,800 pounds of bombs, and a maximum speed of 236 miles per hour. Because of its heavy defensive armament of five machine guns, it was named the Flying Fortress.

Air Corps officials were delighted with the new bomber, but there were no funds for large-scale production and, at that time, no need for a large force of offensive aircraft. A service test quantity of 13 YIB-17's was ordered on January 17, 1936. The first service-model order was placed in 1938, when 38 B-17B's were requested by the Air Corps. Only 13 of these had been delivered by the time war broke out in Europe in 1939.

After the United States became actively involved in the hostilities, 17 Flying Fortresses in the Pacific comprised virtually the only striking force against the Japanese. On December 10, 1941, three of these planes undertook the first American offensive action when they bombed Japanese shipping.

The Model 299 was taken up for its first flight in 1935. The machine went through many design changes.

B-17E's on a routine flight near the Boeing factory in Seattle. Note changes from the earlier Model 299.

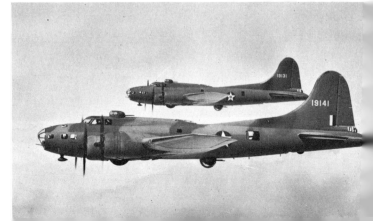

The first American bombing raid against German facilities in Europe was made on August 17, 1942, when 12 Flying Fortresses were sent against the railroad yards at Rouen, France. Not only was the mission a success, but the Fortresses proved their defensive firepower by shooting down four German fighters.

Boeing B-17's roamed far and wide over both the European and Pacific Theatres of Operation. On January 27, 1943, they made the first American attack against Germany itself, when a formation of Fortresses dropped bombs on Wilhelmshaven. On August 17, 1943, they made a spectacular daylight raid against German manufacturing facilities at Schweinfurt, Regensburg, and Wiener Neustadt. Then on March 4, 1944, B-17's were used to make the first American raid on Berlin itself.

A total of 12,731 B-17's had been built by the end of the war. These dropped 640,036 tons of bombs on European targets alone. During its operational life, the plane's bomb load was increased from 4,800 pounds in the Model 299 to 17,600 pounds in the B-17G. At the same time, defensive armament was increased from five .30-caliber machine guns to 13 .50-caliber guns.

Other data (B-17G): Wing span, 103 feet 9 inches; length, 74 feet 4 inches; loaded weight, 65,500 pounds; engines, four 1,200-horsepower Wright Cyclones; maximum speed, 287 miles per hour at 25,000 feet.

11

Above: A combat mission over Europe. Contrails are from escorting fighters. *Below:* The B-17G had two chin guns for extra protection from enemy fighters.

The Hurricane was the R.A.F.'s first standard monoplane fighter. It outfought Germany's bomber force.

Wheel chocks pulled and ready to go. An early model, this Hurricane had been relegated to pilot training.

HAWKER HURRICANE

The name of the Hawker Hurricane will forever be linked to the historic Battle of Britain, which began following the fall of France in June, 1940. Germany's plan was to bomb the British into submission and thus bring an end to the war. However, the final result was the exact opposite. The vaunted German *Luftwaffe* was severely defeated, losing so many of its aircraft that the mass attacks had to be called off. During that bitter struggle, no less than 2,375 German warplanes were destroyed by the outnumbered Royal Air Force Hurricanes and Spitfires—185 of them on a single day.

The origin of the Hurricane can be traced back to October, 1933, when the Royal Air Force decided that a monoplane fighter should be developed to replace the biplanes with which all operational squadrons were equipped. The first experimental model was ordered on February 21, 1935, and the plane was taken into the air for its initial flight on November 6 of the same year. It was the first British military airplane to exceed 300 miles per hour in level flight.

The original Hurricane design called for four .303-caliber machine guns—two synchronized to fire through the propeller arc, and one in each wing. This was changed to eight guns in production models, all of them in the wings. Later versions carried up to 12 guns.

The first production Hurricane Mark 1 was delivered on October 12, 1937. By the time World

War II started, a total of 497 of the fighters had been delivered and formed the main defense of the R.A.F. Fighter Command.

During the first year of the war the Hurricane bore the brunt of fighter operations in Great Britain and was the only monoplane fighter to go into action overseas. The first enemy aircraft shot down by R.A.F. fighters on the Western Front in France was by a Hurricane on October 30, 1939.

In September, 1944, the 12,780th and last Hurricane built in Britain left the production line. Another 1,451 Hurricanes were built in Canada, to a grand total of 14,231. These served with the R.A.F., Fleet Air Arm, and all the Dominion forces. One model, the Hurricane 2D, had two 40-millimeter cannon—the largest guns ever mounted on a single-seat fighter—and was used for low-level attacks against enemy tanks and armored vehicles in North Africa.

The Hurricane also became the first Royal Air Force fighter-bomber, when wing racks to carry two 250-pound bombs were added to the model designated Mark 2B. The first of these "Hurribombers" went into action on October 30, 1941. The bomb load was later increased to two 500 pounders.

The last production version of the Hurricane was the Mark 4, which appeared in March, 1943. The ship could carry two 40-millimeter cannon or eight rockets or up to 1,000 pounds of bombs. It was designed for attacks against ground targets rather than air-to-air fighting and had considerably more armor plate than previous models. These remained in service until October, 1946, when the last Hurricanes were withdrawn.

Other data (Mark 2C): Wing span, 40 feet; length, 32 feet; loaded weight, 7,800 pounds; engine, 1,280-horsepower Rolls-Royce Merlin; maximum speed, 339 miles per hour at 22,000 feet.

A Hurricane 2 with four 20-millimeter cannon. Some models mounted up to 12 machine guns in the wings.

SUPERMARINE SPITFIRE

The official historian of the Battle of Britain records how, during the greatest route of the German *Luftwaffe* on September 15, 1940, when the enemy lost 185 aircraft in combat with the Royal Air Force, the German pilots could be heard calling out warnings to each other over their radios, "*Achtung! Spitfeuer!*"

There is no doubt that German pilots respected the Spitfire more than any other Allied fighter in the early years of the war. And while new and improved enemy aircraft were able to outperform many of the Spitfire variants, that respect continued throughout the war.

The Spitfire owed its heritage to the Schneider Cup Trophy seaplane racer designed by Reginald J. Mitchell for the Supermarine Aviation Works. The first of these, the S-4, was wrecked in 1925 after establishing a new world's speed record of 226.7 miles per hour. The S-5, S-6, and S-6B won the Schneider races in 1927, 1929, and 1931. The S-6B also set a new world's speed record of 407.5 miles per hour. This mark remained unbeaten until April 26, 1939, when a Messerschmitt Me.109R achieved a speed of 469.2 miles per hour.

The first experimental single-seat fighter produced by Supermarine had a fixed landing gear and used the 600-horsepower Rolls-Royce Goshawk engine. While this satisfied the British Air Ministry's requirements, Reginald Mitchell was not satisfied and went back to work at his drawing board. The result was the first true Spitfire, which remained virtually unchanged in external appearance throughout its production life. This test model was taken up for its first flight on March 5, 1936, and it exceeded all expectations.

The Spitfire was ordered into production in June, 1936, and first deliveries were made to the R.A.F. exactly two years later. By the time war was declared, nine squadrons of the Fighter Command had been supplied with the machine.

The Spitfire's guns were fired at German planes

The Spitfire has gone down in the annals of aviation as one of the best single-seat fighters ever built.

for the first time on October 16, 1939, when a formation of 14 Dornier and Heinkel bombers appeared over the Firth of Forth in Scotland. Two of the raiders were shot down—the first enemy airplanes to be defeated in combat over Great Britain since 1918. Five years later—on October 5, 1944—a Spitfire became the first Allied airplane to shoot down a Messerschmitt Me.262 twin-jet fighter.

The Spitfire was the only Allied fighter to remain in production throughout the war. In actual fact, the last Spitfire did not leave the factory until October, 1947. In all its variations, 20,351 Spitfires were built for the Royal Air Force, and almost 2,300 Seafires, the version for aircraft carriers, were delivered to the Royal Navy Fleet Air Arm. About 600 of the planes were used by the U.S. Army Air Forces.

The Spitfire went through numerous changes during its production life. The original Mark 1 mounted the 1,030-horsepower Rolls-Royce Merlin engine and had a speed of 355 miles per hour at 19,000 feet. The final production model during the war, the Mark 21, used the 2,050-horsepower Rolls-Royce Griffon and was capable of 454 miles per hour at 26,000 feet. Of all the various models, the Mark 5 was built in largest numbers.

Other data (Mark 5): Wing span, 36 feet 10 inches; length, 29 feet 11 inches; loaded weight, 6,417 pounds; engine, 1,440-horsepower Rolls-Royce Merlin; maximum speed, 374 miles per hour at 13,000 feet.

15

Two views of the Spitfire 12. This model had clipped wings so it could maneuver better at low altitudes.

BRISTOL BLENHEIM

The Bristol Blenheim created a sensation when it first reached Royal Air Force squadrons in 1937. Until then, bombers had been considered slow, lumbering things designed not for speed but only to carry explosives to enemy targets. However, the Blenheim was faster than any single-seat fighter then serving with the R.A.F.

The Blenheim design went back to 1935, when the Air Ministry requested designs for a high-speed bomber. The plane was ordered into production without a test model; the first production model was taken up for its initial flight on June 25, 1936.

England declared war against Germany at 11:15 A.M. on September 3, 1939. At one minute past noon that day the Royal Air Force Bomber Command flew its first mission of the war, a reconnaissance flight to photograph the German fleet steaming out of Wilhelmshaven. The airplane used on that mission was a Blenheim. The next day ten Blenheims made the first Allied bombing attack against the Germans; five of the bombers failed to return.

Approximately 200 Blenheims were converted to night fighters, with four .303-caliber machine guns under the nose in addition to its single fixed, forward-firing gun. Blenheim Fighters were the first British warplanes to carry radar, and these scored heavily against enemy bombers that tried to come over on nighttime raids.

A Bristol Blenheim at an R.A.F. base in France in 1939. At that time the Blenheim was a first-line bomber.

Above: The Blenheim was produced both with a long nose and short nose. This is the long-nosed model.
Right: A flight of Blenheims wings toward Germany.

A total of 3,482 Blenheims was built. Normal armament was five machine guns. The bomb load consisted of 1,000 pounds internally and 320 pounds on external wing racks.

Other data (Mark 4): Wing span, 56 feet 4 inches; length, 42 feet 7 inches; loaded weight, 13,500 pounds; engines, two 920-horsepower Bristol Mercury XV's; maximum speed, 266 miles per hour at 11,800 feet.

SHORT SUNDERLAND

At the outbreak of war, the Sunderland was the only long-range flying boat in the Royal Air Force. This excellent aircraft had gone into service the previous year, and it remained in first-line operation until January, 1959. This operational life of 21 years was longer than any other airplane had ever served with the R.A.F.

The Air Ministry's initial order for 21 Sunder-

A Short Sunderland races across the water to reach take-off speed. It was Britain's best flying boat.

lands was placed in March, 1936, and the plane was flown for the first time in October, 1937. It was the first British flying boat to have power-operated gun turrets.

To a Sunderland went the credit of destroying the first German submarine by aircraft action. This was on January 30, 1940, when one of the planes damaged a U-boat so badly with bombs that the crew was forced to abandon it.

While the Sunderland was designed primarily for convoy and antisubmarine patrols rather than actual fighting, the plane saw a considerable amount of combat action and proved itself a dangerous opponent. During a patrol over the North Sea on April 3, 1940, a Sunderland was attacked by six German Junkers Ju.88's. The flying boat's gunners shot down one of the enemy planes in flames, forced another to land in Norway, and drove off the remaining four. Later in the war, a Sunderland shot down three of eight attacking Ju.88's.

In 1944, one squadron fitted four machine guns to the noses of their Sunderlands. These were fired by the pilots, who flew the big airplanes like fighters. The fixed guns, plus the two power turrets with four guns each and two waist guns, gave the planes so much firepower that the Germans started calling them "Flying Porcupines."

Short Brothers and other companies produced a total of 689 Sunderlands. These carried up to 2,000 pounds of bombs or depth charges.

Other data (Mark 5): Wing span, 112 feet 9 inches; length, 85 feet 4 inches; loaded weight, 60,000 pounds; engines, four 1,200-horsepower Pratt & Whitney Twin Wasps; maximum speed, 213 miles per hour at 5,000 feet.

Above: A beautiful airplane, the big Sunderland was easy to fly and had a cruising range of 2,900 miles.

Below: This Sunderland has four fixed machine guns in the nose in addition to a power-operated turret.

GRUMMAN F4F WILDCAT

In the 1930's Grumman Aircraft Company became a prime contractor for U.S. Navy fighter planes. Their trim biplane series started with the FF-1 in 1931 and ended with the F3F-3, the last of which was delivered in 1939. While its F3F series was still in production, Grumman built a test model of the F4F Wildcat, which was taken up for its first flight on December 23, 1937. This plane was to become the Navy's first monoplane fighter. Other companies had submitted monoplanes prior to the F4F, but none of these had been ordered.

The F4F was not a notable improvement in speed over the F3F, but it had better firepower, a longer range, and was easier to service because of its all-metal construction. The plane was ordered into limited production in 1940, but it was soon to become the Navy's standard shipboard fighter.

The export model of the F4F was called the G-36, and this was ordered by the British Fleet Air Arm, where it was called the Martlet. Two Martlets won

A flight of Wildcats on the prowl. The Grumman single-seater was more rugged than the faster Japanese Zero.

fame on December 25, 1940, when they became the first American-built airplanes to score in the war, forcing down a German Junkers Ju.88.

When the Japanese struck at Wake Island on December 8, 1941, eight of the 12 Wildcats stationed there were destroyed. The remaining four flew almost constantly for two weeks, sinking a Japanese cruiser and submarine and shooting down six enemy aircraft.

Wildcats were not as fast or as maneuverable as the Japanese Mitsubishi Zeros, but they were more rugged and could absorb tremendous amounts of punishment. This ability made them able to stand up against the more modern enemy fighters. In one raid against the Marshall Islands, a squadron of Wildcats shot down three Japanese bombers and ten fighters without loss to themselves.

Other data (F4F-4): Wing span, 38 feet; length, 28 feet 10 inches; loaded weight, 6,100 pounds; engine, 1,200-horsepower Pratt & Whitney Twin Wasp; maximum speed, 315 miles per hour at 15,000 feet.

To fill the Navy's need for planes, Wildcats were also built by General Motors under the designation FM-2.

DOUGLAS SBD DAUNTLESS

There were few airplanes in World War II which seemed less destined for immortality than the Douglas SBD Dauntless dive bomber. It was slow, poorly armed, and was approaching obsolescence when the Japanese struck at Pearl Harbor in 1941. Despite these drawbacks, it became the backbone of the U.S. Navy's offensive power and established a superior combat record.

The SBD owed its basic design to the Northrop BT-1 of 1934, which in 1938 was modified into the XBT-2. Before the last of these was delivered, the Northrop company became a Douglas subsidiary and the designation was changed to SBD-1.

The Dauntless won its greatest victories against the Japanese during the Battles of the Coral Sea and Midway in May and June, 1942, when six enemy aircraft carriers, three heavy cruisers, five destroyers, and five troop transports were sunk. The Japanese never recovered from these losses.

The SBD carried only two synchronized guns and two swivel guns and was not noted for its maneuverability, yet it had the lowest combat loss of any U.S. Navy airplane. The 5,991st and last SBD was completed in July, 1944. Most of these served with the Navy, though 863 were delivered to the U.S. Army Air Forces as A-24 Banshees.

Other data (SBD-6): Wing span, 41 feet 6 inches; length, 33 feet 1 inch; loaded weight, 9,298 pounds; engine, 1,200-horsepower Wright Cyclone; maximum speed, 254 miles per hour at 17,200 feet.

The Dauntless had the lowest loss ratio of any U.S. Navy plane. This SBD-1 has a bomb under the fuselage.

Above: A flight of SBD's ready to take off from an aircraft carrier. **Above, *right*:** Note the twin guns in the rear cockpit. **Below:** The fuselage markings indicate that this Dauntless had made 23 missions.

CURTISS P-40 HAWK

On July 7, 1937, the Curtiss Aeroplane Company received an order for 210 P-36A Mohawk single-seat fighters. This was the largest peacetime contract the U.S. Army Air Corps had ever awarded for fighters. The tenth production airplane had its engine changed from a Pratt & Whitney radial to an Allison in-line and became the XP-40. This model was first flown in October, 1938, and the following year a contract was issued for 524 of the planes.

With the outbreak of World War II, the Curtiss single-seater was also ordered by the French and

The experimental XP-40 was a production P-36A Mohawk with its radial engine replaced by an in-line.

The Royal Air Force made good use of its Curtiss Hawks in the hard desert campaign in North Africa.

British. The Royal Air Force gave the P-40 a new name: Tomahawk. Improved models were called Kittyhawk and Warhawk.

The P-40 was the only ground-based American fighter to see active combat service throughout the war. When the Japanese launched their first attack against Pearl Harbor on December 7, 1941, 73 P-40's were destroyed on the ground. The following day, when enemy planes attacked the Philippines, four P-40's took off and shot down three of the

24

raiders. P-40's were also the first fighters to serve with American forces in Europe.

P-40 Hawks established their greatest records with General Claire Chennault's American Volunteer Group in China. The Flying Tigers, as they were more popularly known, were the first Americans to participate in the war on the Asian mainland. In a period of only eight months, the Tigers were credited with destroying 286 Japanese planes with the loss of only 23 pilots.

Royal Air Force Hawks were also quite successful. While these did not meet the high-altitude performance requirements necessary in Europe, they performed well in North Africa, where they were used mostly for ground attack.

The original P-40 mounted a 1,040-horsepower Allison engine and had a speed of 357 miles per hour. The final version was the XP-40Q, which appeared in 1945. This model had an engine rated at 1,425 horsepower and was the fastest of the series, with a speed of 442 miles per hour. However, the XP-40Q was not ordered into production.

Other data (P-40N): Wing span, 37 feet 4 inches; length, 33 feet 4 inches; loaded weight, 8,850 pounds; engine, 1,360-horsepower Allison; maximum speed, 378 miles per hour at 10,500 feet.

Top: The P-40F had a Rolls-Royce Merlin engine and a speed of 373 m.p.h. **Center:** A P-40N with a drop tank. **Bottom:** The P-40Q was the last of the series.

Above: The P-38 was the only twin-engined American fighter built during the war. Below: Four machine guns in the nose gave the Lightning a potent punch.

LOCKHEED P-38 LIGHTNING

During the struggle for air supremacy over the Mediterranean during the war, many defeated German pilots who parachuted from their aircraft complained bitterly about *"der Gabelschwanz Teufel."*

The *Gabelschwanz Teufel*, or fork-tailed devil, was the Lockheed P-38 Lightning. Meanwhile, the Lightning was helping to beat back the Japanese in the Pacific, and it was smashing all military precedent by flying directly from the United States to nearly every battlefront—the only U.S. fighter capable of such long-distance flights.

When the design for the P-38 was suggested to

the U.S. Army Air Corps in 1937 as an experimental project, it was considered radical. There had never been a twin-boomed, twin-engined fighter in the history of American military aviation, and the projected loaded weight of 14,800 pounds was heavier than some of the bombers then flying. However, Lockheed was given a contract to proceed with the test model, and it was taken up for its first flight on January 27, 1939.

On February 11, 1939, Lieutenant Ben Kelsey flew the first XP-38 across the country from California to New York, making the trip in seven hours and two minutes. Ironically, Lieutenant Kelsey undershot on his approach to Mitchel Field and crashed, destroying the airplane.

While the P-38 had an excellent record in Europe, it was particularly outstanding in the Pacific area. According to official records, Lightnings brought down more Japanese aircraft than any other land-based fighters. Major Richard Bong, America's ace of aces in the war, claimed all of his 40 Japanese victims while flying a P-38. Just short of his record was Major Thomas McGuire, another P-38 pilot, who scored 38 victories.

A Lightning flown by Lieutenant Colonel Cass Hough established the fastest speed ever attained by a propeller-driven airplane. He dived his craft almost vertically for 25,000 feet, reaching a speed of 780 miles per hour.

Lockheed built a total of 9,924 P-38's. An en-

larged version, the two-seat XP-58 Chain Lightning, was produced in June, 1944. It had a speed of 430 miles per hour but was not put into production.

Other data (P-38L): Wing span, 52 feet; length, 37 feet 10 inches; loaded weight, 21,600 pounds; engines, two 1,475-horsepower Allisons; maximum speed, 414 miles per hour at 25,000 feet.

Final version of the Lightning was the P-38L, which could carry 4,000 pounds of bombs and do 414 m.p.h.

The Yak-1 was similar to the Supermarine Spitfire in general layout. Yakovlev fighters were Russia's best.

YAKOVLEV YAK-3

When Alexsandir Yakovlev evolved the design for his I-26 fighter in the spring of 1939, he was the youngest aircraft designer in the Soviet Union and virtually unknown. But his creation, which was later designated Yak-1, became the first version of what was to become Russia's most successful single-seat fighter.

When the test model of the plane was built, Rus-

sia was extremely short of aluminum alloy for aircraft construction, and Yakovlev was forced to use wood and welded steel tubing. This initial drawback became one of the chief advantages of the Yak fighters. The steel tubing and wood made them easy to produce, and thus deliveries to operational squadrons could be made quickly. By the time hostilities came to an end, more than 20,000 of the planes had been completed.

Yak fighters first appeared in combat during the

Battle of Stalingrad, which started in August, 1942. The plane was a surprise to the Germans. Whereas previously the *Luftwaffe* had enjoyed complete aerial superiority, it now had to contend with a machine that not only had a faster rate of climb than the Messerschmitt Me.109 but could maneuver better at low altitudes.

Improved versions of the Russian fighter came along rapidly, the Yak-9 appearing in 1943. One of these, without military equipment, achieved a speed of 434 miles per hour during acceptance tests. However, this was not the final improved version. For some unexplained reason, the Russians did not always follow the accepted numerical system for indicating improved models. The Yak-3, for example, appeared considerably later than the Yak-9. Yak-3's did not go into squadron service until late in the summer of 1944. The fastest version was the Yak-7, which reached a speed of 447 miles per hour at 18,860 feet.

Other data (Yak-3): Wing span, 30 feet 2 inches; length, 28 feet; loaded weight, 5,864 pounds; engine, 1,260-horsepower Klimov; maximum speed, 403 miles per hour at 16,400 feet.

Yak-9's at an operational field. One test model achieved a speed of 434 m.p.h. without military equipment.

SHORT STIRLING

The Stirling was the smallest of the Royal Air Force's "big three" four-engined bombers of World War II. However, it established several important firsts in R.A.F. history. It was the first four-engined all-metal monoplane ever ordered, the first to be powered by air-cooled rather than liquid-cooled engines, and it comprised the first four-engined bomber squadron of the war. The first Stirlings to go into operation carried a greater bomb load than the early B-17 Flying Fortresses and also more defensive guns.

By 1935 the British Air Ministry realized that its biplane bombers required replacement, and in July of the following year manufacturers were requested to submit plans for a new machine with a higher speed and the ability to carry heavier loads of bombs. Short Brothers won the competition with their Stirling design. For several years the company had been specializing in flying boats, and this was the first bomber it had ever designed.

The first test model of the Stirling made its initial flight in May, 1939, but crashed on landing. The second test machine was ready shortly after the outbreak of hostilities, and it was ordered into immediate production.

Stirlings went into action for the first time on February 10, 1941, when four of the machines dropped 56 500-pound bombs on Rotterdam, Holland. Two months later—April 17—they struck at Berlin with the heaviest bombs that had been dropped on the German capital. The longest mission flown by Stirlings was against the famed Skoda armament factory in Pilsen, Czechoslovakia.

The Stirling had the heaviest defensive firepower of any bomber in the world when it went into service, with four machine guns in the tail turret and four others in the nose and top fuselage turrets. It carried a maximum load of 14,000 pounds of bombs on short raids or 3,500 pounds over a range of 2,010 miles.

Other data (Mark 3): Wing span, 99 feet 1 inch; length, 87 feet 3 inches; loaded weight, 70,000 pounds; engines, four 1,650-horsepower Bristol Hercules; maximum speed, 267 miles per hour at 14,500 feet.

Flying in close formation such as this, Short Stirlings could put up concentrated defensive firepower.

30

Above: A Stirling being made ready for a night-time mission. According to British experience, daylight bombing raids were too expensive in terms of machines lost.

Right: The job of loading a Stirling required a long time. The bomber could carry up to seven tons on short missions or 3,500 pounds to targets deep in Germany.

HANDLEY-PAGE HALIFAX

In May, 1918, the largest airplane built in England during World War I was taken into the air for the first time. This was the Handley-Page V/1500, the first four-engined R.A.F. bomber, which had been designed to strike at Berlin from home bases in Great Britain. The war came to a close before this advanced airplane could be put into squadron operation.

The vision of the strategic possibilities of the V/1500 was finally realized in the Halifax, which was the second of Britain's four-engined monoplane bombers to enter service in World War II but the first such warplane to drop bombs on Germany.

The origins of the Halifax can be traced back to an Air Ministry request to manufacturers in September, 1936, for an all-metal medium-heavy bomber. The plane was originally designed for two engines, but this was later increased to four. Two test models were ordered on September 3, 1937. Before the first of these was delivered, another 100 were ordered.

The first experimental Halifax was taken up for its maiden flight on October 25, 1939, and its performance was excellent. By that time war had been declared, and the bomber was ordered into volume production by four aircraft companies in addition to Handley-Page.

A flight of six Halifaxes went on their first offensive mission on March 10, 1941, with a strike against the port facilities at Le Havre, France. From then on the plane started hitting enemy targets in ever-increasing numbers. The most devastating attacks in which the Halifaxes participated were those of July, 1943, against the city of Hamburg. British aircraft dropped 2,300 tons of bombs on Hamburg in the first of these saturation raids, causing the greatest fires in history and virtually destroying the city and its war potential.

An early version of the Halifax. Later models had four guns in the tail, two on top of the fuselage.

Halifaxes made some of the longest R.A.F. raids of the war. The deepest of these penetrations was against important aircraft engine and armament factories in Milan, Italy.

In addition to bombing, Halifaxes were sent on numerous specialized missions. These included towing gliders for invasion of France, dropping secret agents and supplies, and jamming enemy radio communications.

The Handley-Pages were used mostly for nighttime operations, but in 1944 they went back to daytime missions, striking German V-1 "buzz-bomb" sites and airfields. In June, 1944, one Halifax squadron shot down 33 German fighters, which was a Bomber Command record for a single month.

A total of 6,176 Halifaxes was built. These made 75,532 sorties against enemy targets and dropped 227,610 tons of bombs. The plane's maximum bomb load was 14,500 pounds, and normal armament consisted of nine .303-caliber machine guns.

Other data (Mark 5): Wing span, 104 feet 2 inches; length, 71 feet 7 inches; loaded weight, 68,-000 pounds; engines, four 1,390-horsepower Rolls-Royce Merlins; maximum speed, 265 miles per hour at 17,500 feet.

An unglamorous workhorse, the Stirling carried on a tradition which Handley-Page had started in World War I.

CONSOLIDATED B-24 LIBERATOR

The Liberator was one of the finest airplanes to see action in World War II. Though somewhat slower than the lighter B-17 Flying Fortress and with a lower service ceiling, it had a considerably longer operational range, a larger bomb capacity, and was one of the most rugged airplanes ever produced.

Design work on the project was begun in response to a U.S. Army Air Corps request early in 1939 for a bomber with better performance than the B-17. The first XB-24 was designed and built in exactly eight months, and was taken up for its first flight on December 29, 1939. This plane later became the XB-24B, after self-sealing fuel tanks, heavier armor, and turbosuperchargers had been added.

The Air Corps proceeded slowly in development of the B-24, but the French Government placed an order for 120 of the machines. When France collapsed, the British Royal Air Force took over the order. The first R.A.F. Liberator was completed on January 17, 1941. Additional British orders brought the total number supplied to 1,694.

Liberators went into action with American units in Europe for the first time on October 9, 1942, with an attack against German targets in Lille, France. Within a few months, B-24's were hitting installations deep in enemy territory that had previously been safe from Allied bombs.

34

Above: **Liberators of the Eighth Air Force dropping sticks of bombs over Germany.** *Below:* **Waist gunners on a B-24 prepare their weapons for aerial combat.**

The most notable of all the long-range Liberator missions were those against the Ploesti oil refinery in Romania, which was one of the largest suppliers of gasoline for the Germans. The first of these attacks was made by 12 B-24's on June 11, 1942. While the operation proved the long-range capabilities of the plane, the attack itself caused comparatively little damage.

Liberators were sent against Ploesti again on August 1, 1943, and this time the mission was a success. Taking off from Libya in North Africa, 177 B-24's flew low across the Mediterranean and blasted the Ploesti refinery. The round-trip flight was 2,700 miles, and it was made without fighter escort. However, 57 of the raiders were lost, making it one of the most costly American missions of the war. Five of the crewmen were awarded Congressional Medals of Honor.

More Liberators were built during the war than any other single type of American airplane. A total of 18,190 B-24's left the production line, while cargo and U.S. Navy PB4Y-1 versions brought the final production figure to 19,251. U.S. Air Force models alone flew 312,734 sorties and dropped 634,831 tons of bombs.

Other data (B-24J): Wing span, 110 feet; length, 67 feet 2 inches; loaded weight, 65,000 pounds; engines, four 1,200-horsepower Pratt & Whitney Twin Wasps; maximum speed, 294 miles per hour at 25,000 feet.

35

Above: The B-24J was built in larger numbers than any other Liberator model. *Below:* The last production type was the B-24M, which could do 215 m.p.h.

HAWKER TYPHOON

While the Hawker Typhoon was originally designed as an interceptor fighter, it fell short of the performance qualities required for such duties. However, the plane went on to achieve notable success as a tactical fighter during the Allied advances through France and Holland in 1944.

The Typhoon had a long development history. It was designed to mount the 2,000-horsepower Napier Sabre engine, and the experimental model was taken up for its first flight on February 24, 1940. The plane was expected to be in squadron service within a few months, but Napier was unable to perfect its new engine quickly enough. The first production aircraft did not fly until May 26, 1941, and service models started to go to R.A.F. squadrons two months later.

Pilots were at first enthusiastic about the Typhoon. It was the first R.A.F. fighter capable of flying in excess of 400 miles per hour, which was enough to match the new German single-seaters. But despite this high speed, the Napier engine was unreliable, the plane's rate of climb was inferior, and its high-altitude performance disappointing. These problems, plus structural weakness in the tail, caused R.A.F.

Bristling with guns and rockets, a Typhoon is made ready for a mission from an R.A.F. field in France after the invasion. The plane could do 405 m.p.h.

officials to consider withdrawing the machine from first-line service.

The tail problems were altered and mechanics learned better methods to service the engine. With these difficulties solved, the Typhoon was used for low-level sweeps—and suddenly it became an outstanding success. The planes were sent over France against German trains, and they destroyed an average of 150 locomotives a month. They also put a stop to low-level raids by German Focke-Wulf Fw.190's, which no other Royal Air Force fighters could match for speed.

A further development of the Typhoon was called the Tempest, which went into production in 1943. This was the fastest propeller-driven airplane delivered to the British military during the war, with a maximum speed of 427 miles per hour. Tempests established an outstanding record by destroying 638 German V-1 jet-propelled "buzz-bombs." Operating from bases in Holland and Belgium, they also shot down 20 Messerschmitt Me.262 jet fighters.

Other data (Typhoon 1B): Wing span, 41 feet 7 inches; length, 31 feet 11 inches; loaded weight, 11,400 pounds; engine, 2,180-horsepower Napier Sabre IIB; maximum speed, 405 miles per hour at 18,000 feet.

Three views of the Typhoon. Normal armament consisted of four 20-millimeter cannon in the wings and eight 60-pound rockets. 3,330 Typhoons were built.

MIKOYAN-GUREVICH MIG-3

When the Germans turned their armed might against Russia on June 22, 1941, the Red Air Force was not ready for war. Newer types of aircraft were in production, but none of these had reached operational squadrons in appreciable numbers. At that time, the mainstay fighters were still the old I-15 biplane and I-16 monoplane, both of which had been created in 1933 by a design team under Nikolai Polikarpov. These planes had fought well in the Spanish Civil War, which started in 1936, but they were obsolete by the time Russia became embroiled in World War II and were shot down in large numbers by superior German fighters.

Russia had previously realized that its air force was inadequate and that its first-line aircraft required replacement. Requests for new designs were sent out to engineers, among whom were Artem Mikoyan and Mikhail Gurevich, who had formed a design team. Neither had previously designed a single-seat fighter, but their MiG-1 seemed to have all the characteristics of an excellent machine.

When the test model was taken up for its first flight on April 5, 1940, the pilot reported that while the plane was extremely fast, it was tricky to fly and had a very high landing speed. Mikoyan and Gurevich were requested to correct these problems. They were also instructed to add a canopy instead of continuing with an open-cockpit design. Despite these drawbacks, the MiG-1 was considered such an advancement in Soviet fighters that it won a Stalin prize for its designers.

Production of the plane had begun even before the desired changes were made. The improved model was called the MiG-3, and required alterations were made right on the factory floor so that there would be no interruption in production. The MiG-3 had cleaner lines than the former model, and while handling characteristics were improved, the plane was still tricky to fly.

MiG-3's did not achieve the prominence of the Yak fighters. However, they served their purpose by helping to lower the huge combat losses which had been suffered by pilots flying the earlier fighter designs.

Normal armament consisted of two 7.6-millimeter machine guns on top of the fuselage and one 12.7-millimeter gun below the engine. These were all synchronized to fire through the propeller arc. Some planes also had one 12.7-millimeter gun fitted in each wing.

Production of the MiG-3 came to an end late in 1941 when its engine was discontinued in favor of engines for the Iluyshin Il-2 Stormovik. A total of 2,100 MiG-1's and MiG-3's was built.

Other data (MiG-3): Wing span, 33 feet 9 inches; length, 26 feet 9 inches; loaded weight, 7,695 pounds; engine, 1,350-horsepower Mikulin; maximum speed, 378 miles per hour at 22,960 feet.

While the MiG-3 had pleasing lines and was one of the fastest Russian single-seaters, it was tricky to fly and was not a favorite among pilots. Despite these drawbacks, it was effective in aerial combat.

Above: Corsairs were the largest and heaviest fighters in the U.S. Navy. *Below:* This picture was made as an F4U left a carrier. Note auxiliary fuel tank.

VOUGHT F4U CORSAIR

Few military airplanes can boast the record of the Vought F4U Corsair, which proved the excellence of its design by remaining in service longer than any other American combat plane. The XF4U-1 was originally designed in 1938 and was taken up for its first flight on May 29, 1940. The plane remained in constant production until February, 1953, when the 12,571st and last Corsair was rolled off the production line.

The bent-wing design of the airplane was decided

40

upon so that it could swing the huge propeller for its 2,000-horsepower engine and still use a short landing gear. This was the most powerful engine that had ever been installed in a fighter. As a result of its brute power, the Corsair became the world's first military plane to exceed 400 miles per hour in level flight with a full combat load.

U.S. Marines were the first pilots to take the Corsair into action. This was on February 14, 1943, when they flew out of Guadalcanal to escort Navy patrol bombers on a mission to Bougainville in the Solomon Islands.

F4U's established a combat record that was beyond compare, shooting down a total of 2,140 enemy aircraft for a combat loss of only 189. This was a victory ratio of better than 11.3 to one!

While the Corsair had been designed as a fighter, it was also used as a dive bomber. During one mission against the Japanese, an F4U went out with 4,000 pounds of bombs—the heaviest load ever carried to that time by a single-engined fighter.

Other data (F4U-4): Wing span, 40 feet 11 inches; length, 33 feet 8 inches; loaded weight, 12,785 pounds; engine, 2,100-horsepower Pratt & Whitney Double Wasp; maximum speed, 451 miles per hour at 19,500 feet.

Top: The eye-pleasing F4U was the fastest of Navy fighters. **Center:** Marine Corsairs head out for a patrol. **Bottom:** At an island base in the Pacific.

NORTH AMERICAN B-25 MITCHELL

The B-25 Mitchell has been called the most versatile of all American combat airplanes in World War II. While the plane was originally designed as a medium bomber, it was also used for ground strafing, photo reconnaissance, submarine patrol, and even as a fighter. One version became the most heavily-armed airplane ever built.

Design work on the project was started in 1938 in answer to an Army Air Corps request for a medium bomber. North American was given a contract for one test model of the plane, and this was flown for the first time in January, 1939. After an engine change, the prototype was delivered to the Army for testing, and a short time later it was destroyed in a crash. This machine did not have a military designation but was known as the NA-40.

As a result of its brief test program, the Air Corps awarded North American a contract for one XB-25, though with a number of changes from the original. This plane was completed on August 19, 1940, and it was considerably improved over the NA-40. In addition to other changes, the loaded weight was increased from 19,500 pounds in the NA-40 to 27,310 pounds in the XB-25. The airplane was named Mitchell in honor of General William Mitchell, the American air power advocate of World War I and the years immediately following the war.

The B-25 Mitchell first made headlines on April

The original XB-25 was completed in August, 1940. It was an improved version of the North American NA-40.

18, 1942, when a flight of 16 of the planes under the command of Lieutenant Colonel James Doolittle took off from the aircraft carrier *Hornet* and carried the first American air attack of the war to Japan itself, striking Tokyo, Yokohama, and other important industrial cities. The plan had been for the B-25's to fly to bases in China, but they ran out of fuel and were unable to reach their intended destinations. All of the planes were lost and most of the crews captured, but an important psychological blow had been struck against the Japanese homeland.

Normal armament on the B-25C and D models was six .50-caliber machine guns plus 3,000 pounds of bombs. However, in 1944 the B-25H became the most heavily armed airplane in the world, with 14 .50-caliber guns and a 75-millimeter cannon. This model was for use against enemy shipping in the Pacific. The B-25J, which also appeared in 1944, had eight .50-caliber guns in the nose in addition to four turrets with six guns.

North American produced almost 11,000 B-25's, 9,816 of which were for the Army Air Forces while the remainder were flown by the Dutch, British, Chinese, Russian, and Australian air forces.

Other data (B-25J): Wing span, 67 feet 7 inches; length, 52 feet 11 inches; loaded weight, 35,000 pounds; engines, two 1,700-horsepower Wright Cyclones; maximum speed, 275 miles per hour at 13,000 feet.

43

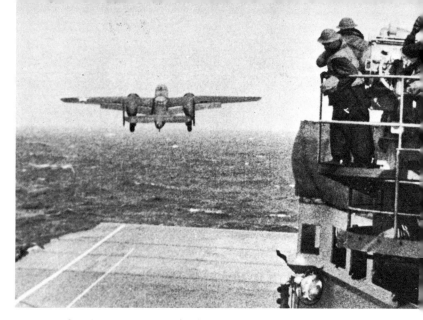

Above: The first of 16 Mitchells takes off from the carrier *Hornet* to bomb Japan. *Below:* The B-25H had a 75-millimeter cannon as well as 14 machine guns.

Engineers weigh one of the first Mustangs for the R.A.F. It had four wing guns, two synchronized guns.

The Mustang with Royal Air Force markings. Some pilots at first mistook it for a German Messerschmitt.

NORTH AMERICAN P-51 MUSTANG

Late in April, 1940, the British Purchasing Commission asked the North American Aviation company to build a single-seat fighter for the Royal Air Force that had been designed by another company. However, North American informed the Commission that it would prefer to design an entirely new airplane, incorporating lessons which had been learned in the first months of the war. The British gave their permission, on the condition that the first test model would be ready within 120 days.

This was a bold proposal for North American, since the firm had never built a successful fighter. Their engineers and mechanics worked around the

clock, and the new design, called the NA-73, was ready in 117 days. After testing, the plane was ordered into immediate production.

While the British were responsible for bringing the Mustang into existence, the plane won its greatest fame with the U.S. Army Air Forces, shooting down more enemy aircraft than any other American fighter in the European Theatre. The final tally showed seven enemy planes destroyed for every P-51 lost in combat.

P-51B's went into operation in Europe on December 13, 1943. On January 15, 1944, they became the first American fighter planes to cross the German border, and in March they started flying escort all the way to Berlin with B-17 and B-24 bombers. The

Mustangs were able to fly such long missions through the aid of two 110-gallon wing fuel tanks. These tanks were dropped as soon as the gasoline they contained had been consumed.

Other data (P-51D): Wing span, 37 feet; length, 32 feet 3 inches; loaded weight, 11,600 pounds; engine, 1,490-horsepower Rolls-Royce Merlin; maximum speed, 437 miles per hour at 25,000 feet.

Right: P-51D's at an operational field in England. Note individual aircraft markings. *Below:* A flight of Mustangs with wing drop tanks starts on a mission.

179 was considered the best design submitted, and in September, 1939, the Air Corps ordered 1,100 of the machines into production without an experimental model.

The first B-26 was taken up for its maiden test flight on November 25, 1940, and it exceeded all performance expectations. With two 1,850-horsepower Pratt & Whitney Double Wasp engines, it had a maximum speed of 315 miles per hour; the plane could carry 5,800 pounds of bombs, and its loaded weight was 30,035 pounds. However, it had a very

B-26's could take a great amount of punishment. This one was badly shot up, yet it returned to its base.

Smoothly streamlined, the Martin Marauder was the fastest medium bomber in the U.S. Army Air Forces.

MARTIN B-26 MARAUDER

The B-26 Marauder was one of the most controversial American airplanes of World War II. The crews either hated it or loved it; they either finished their missions safely or washed out quickly. An unforgiving airplane, the Marauder was excellent in the hands of a skilled pilot or a deathtrap to one who was inexperienced.

The B-26 came into being through an Air Corps request to manufacturers on January 25, 1939, calling for a fast medium bomber carrying a bomb load of 2,000 pounds and four machine guns. The Martin

high landing speed and was considered dangerous for most pilots just out of the student stage. In an effort to correct this, a longer wing was installed. This change also lowered the plane's performance.

B-26's went into action in Europe for the first time on May 14, 1943, when a flight of 11 of the machines made a low-level attack against the generating plant at Ijmuiden, Holland. Not one of the Marauders returned.

Despite this disastrous first showing, the B-26 earned the record of being the safest Allied bomber

Marauders often went out alone, but this one has a Republic P-47 Thunderbolt flying escort over France.

in the war. Its final combat loss was less than one-half of 1 per cent, and more than 250 Marauders completed 100 missions each. One of these, *Flak Bait*, was the first Allied bomber to complete 100 missions.

The Martin Company produced a total of 5,266 B-26's. These flew more than 110,000 sorties and dropped 150,000 tons of bombs.

Other data (B-25G): Wing span, 71 feet; length, 56 feet 1 inch; loaded weight, 38,200 pounds; engines, two 2,000-horsepower Pratt & Whitney Double Wasps; maximum speed, 305 miles per hour at 15,000 feet.

A graphic example of precision bombing. Marauders have just hit the hangars of a German bomber base.

47

DE HAVILLAND MOSQUITO

Just as the De Havilland DH-4 was one of the best and most talked-about bombers of World War I, so the Mosquito from the same company achieved outstanding success in World War II. It was the only all-wood combat plane produced by the Allies, and when the Mosquito first went into service it was the fastest operational airplane in the world.

The Mosquito was conceived as a high-speed unarmed bomber capable of outdistancing all likely pursuers. Wooden construction was decided upon to simplify design and to conserve aluminum for other aircraft. Design work was started by De Havilland as a private venture in October, 1938. The British Air Ministry did not give official sanction to the project until December, 1939.

The first unarmed bomber version was taken up for its maiden flight on November 25, 1940, and the fighter version was flown for the first time on May 15, 1941. Both of these models were capable of flying almost 400 miles per hour.

The first Mosquitos to see active war service were photo-reconnaissance versions. One of these flew over Occupied France on its initial sortie on September 20, 1941. Three Messerschmitt Me.109 fighters tried to intercept it, but they were unable to match the Mosquito's speed.

Bomber versions went into action for the first time on May 31, 1942, when they made a daylight attack on Cologne, Germany, with 500-pound bombs. On September 25, 1942, four Mosquitos went on a daring flight across the North Sea to Oslo, Norway, where they bombed and machine-gunned the Gestapo headquarters. Some Mosquitos were also sent against Berlin, carrying the 4,000-pound "blockbuster" bombs.

Mosquitos carried the heaviest armament of any British plane in the war. The Mark 6 had four 20-millimeter cannon and four .303-caliber machine guns. Others mounted a 57-millimeter cannon. The 6,439th and last Mosquito built in England was completed in November, 1950. Total Mosquito production, including those made in Canada and Australia, was 7,781.

Other data (Mark 6): Wing span, 54 feet 2 inches; length, 40 feet 6 inches; loaded weight, 22,300 pounds; engines, two 1,230-horsepower Rolls-Royce Merlins; maximum speed, 380 miles per hour at 13,000 feet.

The Mosquito was built entirely of wood. The plane was so fast it could outdistance enemy interceptors.

Unarmed Mosquito bombers depended upon speed alone defense. They made some of the war's most daring ra

AVRO LANCASTER

Of all the heavy bombers to serve with the Royal Air Force during the war, the Avro Lancaster was unquestionably the most outstanding. It carried a greater load of bombs than any other British airplane, and did so with astonishing safety for the crew. According to official records, 132 tons of bombs were dropped for every Lancaster lost in operation. By comparison, only 56 tons were dropped for each Handley-Page Halifax lost, and 41 tons for each Short Stirling.

Except for a stroke of good fortune, it is possible that the Lancaster might never have come into existence. In 1939 the A. V. Roe company produced a twin-engine, all-metal bomber called the Manchester. While the plane handled well, it was an operational failure. This was because its new 1,760-horsepower Rolls-Royce Vulture engines had not been perfected and gave constant trouble. The planes were withdrawn from Bomber Command squadrons in June, 1942, even though the R.A.F. was hard-pressed for equipment.

During 1940 someone thought of putting larger wings on the Manchester and replacing its original engines with four 1,145-horsepower Rolls-Royce Merlins. This test model, called the Manchester III (actually the first Lancaster, as the plane was later renamed), was flown for the first time on January 9, 1941, and was an instant success. The test pilot wrote in his report, "The performance and handling characteristics with full load surpass those of any other bomber."

Lancasters went into operation on March 3, 1942, when four of the planes were sent on a mine-laying mission. They were first used as bombers on March 10, when two Lancasters took part in a raid on Essen, Germany. As the planes became available in

The Lancaster was the heaviest of all R.A.F. bombers. It could carry bombs weighing up to 22,000 pounds.

large numbers, they were sent on massed raids deep into Germany.

Lancasters were capable of lifting exceptionally heavy loads. They dropped the first 8,000-pound bombs and the first 12,000-pound bombs. On March 14, 1945, a Lancaster also dropped the heaviest bomb of the war—the 22,000-pound "Grand Slam."

A. V. Roe and other companies produced a total of 6,834 Lancasters. These flew more than 156,000 sorties and dropped 608,612 tons of bombs. The last Lancaster was not withdrawn from first-line service until February, 1954.

Other data (Mark 3): Wing span, 102 feet; length, 69 feet 6 inches; loaded weight, 70,000 pounds; engines, four 1,640-horsepower Rolls-Royce Merlins; maximum speed, 287 miles per hour at 11,500 feet.

Lancasters had ten machine guns for defensive armament, making them dangerous for enemy fighters to attack.

REPUBLIC P-47 THUNDERBOLT

The P-47 Thunderbolt, or "Jug" as it was more affectionately called, was undoubtedly the roughest, toughest, and most dependable single-seat fighter that flew on either side during World War II. Fully loaded, it weighed almost as much as a bomber, yet it could flip and turn with the ease of a fighter half its size and weight. No other plane could match it as an all-around workhorse.

The story of the Thunderbolt began in the spring of 1940, when the Germans used their air power with telling effect to force the surrender of France in just 40 days. At that time Republic Aviation had a contract to produce the P-43 Lancer and was working on the first model of a small, light fighter called the P-44. However, in the light of events in Europe, the U.S. Army Air Corps decided that something larger and faster would be required.

Alexander Kartveli was Republic Aviation's chief designer, and overnight he prepared a rough sketch of the P-47. It was to have the largest engine ever installed in a single-seat fighter, eight .50-caliber machine guns, and heavy armor plating to protect the pilot. These features added up to an airplane weighing almost seven tons—some 4,000 pounds more than any American fighter in existence.

Engineering work on the P-47 design was exten-

The ground crew services a Thunderbolt on D-Day so it can go on another sortie over the German lines.

This P-47 was badly hit by ground fire over France, but the pilot managed to fly back to his home base.

sive, since the machine had many requirements which were entirely new to American designers. However, the first model, the XP-47B, was ready for flight testing on May 6, 1941. Lowry Brabham was the test pilot, and after just one flight in the new plane he reported enthusiastically, "Boy, we've hit the jackpot!"

P-47's went into operation for the first time on April 8, 1943, flying escort to B-17 bombers and undertaking fighter sweeps. Within a short time they started proving their ruggedness and dependability as well as their fighting ability.

In some two and a half years of wartime operation, Thunderbolts flew more than 546,000 combat sorties, dropped 132,000 tons of bombs, and fired 135 million rounds of ammunition and 60,000 rockets. They destroyed or damaged 11,874 enemy aircraft, 86,000 railroad cars, 9,000 locomotives, and 6,000 armored vehicles and tanks. A total of 15,579 Thunderbolts left the production lines; of these, 5,222 were lost in combat.

Other data (P-47N): Wing span, 42 feet 7 inches; length, 36 feet 1 inch; loaded weight, 20,700 pounds; engine, 2,800-horsepower Pratt & Whitney Double Wasp; maximum speed, 467 miles per hour at 32,500 feet.

Top: The Thunderbolt was huge for a single-seater, but it was one of the best American fighters of the war. *Bottom:* Last production model was the P-47N.

53

An Avenger dropping its torpedo. The machine could carry the largest airborne torpedo used in the war.

GRUMMAN TBF AVENGER

TBF Avengers went into war action for the first time on June 3, 1942, during the historic Battle of Midway. This baptism of fire was a disaster. Of the six Avengers that went against the powerful Japanese fleet, five were shot down by enemy fighters and antiaircraft. It was something of a miracle that the one surviving TBF managed to struggle back, for one of its crewmembers was dead, another wounded, and the plane so shot up it was barely flyable. Against this loss, the Avengers did not score one hit on the Japanese vessels. Despite this poor first showing, the Avenger later became one of the most successful U.S. Navy aircraft of the war.

When the United States entered the war its prime torpedo bomber was the Douglas TBD Devastator, which was obsolete and unable to fight off superior enemy aircraft. The Navy realized this weakness in torpedo bombers before the country became engaged in hostilities, and specifications were laid down for a replacement. The Grumman design was selected, and two test models were ordered on April 8, 1940, the first of which was taken up for its maiden flight on August 1, 1941. Before the first XTBF-1 was completed, 286 of the planes were ordered.

Actual war experience proved that both fighters and torpedo bombers would be required in larger numbers than Grumman would be able to produce in one plant. General Motors had previously been contracted to build the Grumman Wildcat fighter, with the designations FM-1 and FM-2. Now the automobile company's aircraft division was also pressed into building the Avenger under the designation TBM. Grumman production of the Avenger stopped early in 1944, after 2,290 of the planes had been built. The remainder of the program was turned over to General Motors, which produced 2,882 TBM-1's and 4,664 improved TBM-3's.

The Avenger carried a crew of three: pilot, gunner, and radar operator-gunner. The TBF had one synchronized .30-caliber gun, one .30-caliber gun in the lower fuselage, and a .50-caliber gun in the power turret. The forward arrangement was later changed to two .50-caliber guns. The plane could also carry one 1,921-pound torpedo internally or up to 2,000 pounds of bombs.

The Avenger was the largest U.S. Navy plane that had ever been designed for operations from aircraft carriers. However, it had such a low landing speed that deck operations presented no problems.

The Avenger remained operational with the fleet until June, 1954, after which it was transferred to land bases.

Other data (TBM-3E): Wing span, 54 feet 2 inches; length, 40 feet 11 inches; loaded weight, 17,895 pounds; engine, 1,900-horsepower Wright Double Cyclone; maximum speed, 276 miles per hour at 16,500 feet.

Above: The TBF Avenger was the largest plane that had been designed for aircraft carrier operations. **Below:** The deck officer signals a pilot to take off.

ILYUSHIN IL-2 STORMOVIK

An important change took place in the fighting between Russia and Germany when the Ilyushin Il-2 Stormovik started going to front-line squadrons in the spring of 1942. Prior to that time, the German tanks had operated virtually with no aerial opposition; suddenly they were being destroyed in large numbers by the new plane, which was termed an assault bomber.

One of the most heavily armored planes of the war, the Stormovik's entire engine was protected by 6-millimeter armor plate, while the cockpit was surrounded by 13-millimeter plating and also had a bulletproof windscreen and canopy. As further protection, the pilot could raise an armored frame in front of his face before a low-level sweep. This all added up to give the Il-2 the lowest combat loss ratio of any Russian plane.

The Stormovik's normal armament consisted of two 20-millimeter cannon and up to four machine guns. However, its devastating attacks against tanks were made not with guns but with the first armor-piercing rockets carried by aircraft. These weighed 56 pounds each, and four were usually carried below each wing.

The Russians worked out specialized tactics for the Stormovik. Instead of attacking from the front, they circled behind the German tanks and hit them from the rear, where the armor was thinnest. This method of attack also permitted any damaged aircraft to glide safely behind their own lines.

But while the plane was difficult to bring down from the front, it was vulnerable from the rear. To correct this difficulty, the Stormovik design was altered in 1942 to provide a rear gunner. This version was called the Il-3. The gunner had only a single swivel 12.7-millimeter gun, but this was enough to offer adequate protection from the rear. With the rear gun, the Stormovik's loss ratio dropped even lower than previously.

The Stormovik was designed in 1940 by Sergei Ilyushin, and the Russian Army officials were so pleased with the test model that Ilyushin was awarded the Stalin prize of 200,000 rubles. Ironically, however, the basic design of the plane was actually borrowed from the German Heinkel He.118, which was first flown in the spring of 1937. While the Heinkel was not placed in production for the German *Luftwaffe*, manufacturing rights were sold both to Japan and Russia. The Il-2 Stormovik was almost identical in general layout.

The Stormovik was continued in production for several years following the war. The last model was the Il-10, which served in Korea against the United Nations forces.

Other data (Il-3): Wing span, 47 feet 10 inches; length, 38 feet; loaded weight, 12,250 pounds; engine, 1,600-horsepower Mikulin; maximum speed, 257 miles per hour at 6,500 feet.

Stormoviks warm up for a mission. Called an assault bomber, the plane was effective against enemy tanks.

While it was originally designed as a single-seater, a gunner was later added to protect the tail section.

The Superfortress carried the heaviest bomb load of any U.S. plane in the war, and could fly the farthest.

BOEING B-29 SUPERFORTRESS

When World War II broke out in Europe, the U.S. Army Air Corps realized that if the United States was drawn into the conflict a bomber would be required with a greater load-carrying ability than either the Boeing B-17 or Consolidated B-24. Calls were sent out to major aircraft manufacturers on January 29, 1940, requesting a bomber capable of carrying 2,000 pounds of bombs over a range of 5,333 miles or 16,000 pounds over 1,000 miles. Of the four designs submitted, that by Boeing was considered the best. Two test models were ordered on August 24, 1940.

Even before the first XB-29 was taken into the air for its initial flight on September 21, 1941, a total of 1,514 of the machines had been ordered.

Deliveries to service squadrons began in the fall of 1943. Meanwhile, the decision was made not to use the new planes in Europe but to concentrate their employment against the Japanese.

B-29's went into action for the first time on June 5, 1944. Taking off from bases in India, they bombed Japanese targets in Bangkok, Thailand, and continued on to land in China. Ten days later, in the second B-29 operation, the planes were sent against the Japanese mainland. The greatest Superfortress operation was on August 6, 1945, when 801 of the big long-range bombers struck Japan in a single night.

B-29's also dropped the first atomic bombs to be used in warfare. The first of these hit the Japanese city of Hiroshima on August 6, 1945. Seven Superfortresses were sent on the mission, but only one of these carried an atomic bomb. Three days later a second atomic bomb was dropped on Nagasaki. As a direct result of these devastating raids, World War II came to an end on August 14 when Japan surrendered.

Boeing and other manufacturers delivered 3,970 Superfortresses during the war. These dropped a total of 171,060 tons of bombs on Japan compared to 6,781 tons by all other aircraft.

Other data (B-29B): Wing span, 141 feet 3 inches; length, 99 feet; loaded weight, 137,500 pounds; engines, four 2,200-horsepower Wright Cyclones; maximum speed, 368 miles per hour at 25,000 feet.

Incendiary bombs rain earthward from the bomb bays of B-29's during a mission against the big industrial city of Yokohama.

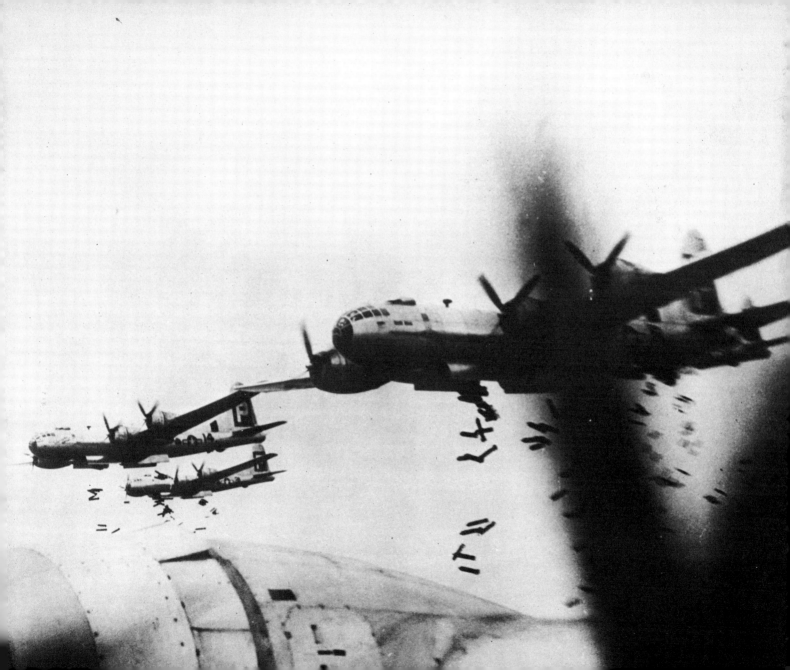

GRUMMAN F6F HELLCAT

When Vice-Admiral Rikizo Tada, Chief of the Japanese Navy Research and Development Center, was interrogated by American naval officers following World War II, he gave the Grumman F6F Hellcat the greatest possible praise. "It was the Grumman Hellcat which beat Japan," he said. "When our High Command finally decided to put into mass production a plane to compete with your F6F, it was too late."

The Hellcat was designed as a replacement for the earlier F4F Wildcat, which fell far short of the performance standards of the Japanese Mitsubishi Zero. But while the Hellcat resembled the Wildcat, it was not merely an improved version of the same basic design. It was not only larger and faster than its predecessor but far more maneuverable and capable of a higher ceiling.

The experimental model of the F6F was flown for the first time in August, 1942, and by December of the same year it was in assembly-line production. The plane had its baptism of fire in September, 1943. When Japanese pilots saw the Hellcats for the first time they thought they were Wildcats and engaged them accordingly. However, they were soon surprised to learn that the new Grumman fighters could not only outmaneuver them but were also

While the Hellcat resembled the earlier F4F Wildcat, it was larger, faster, and had a much better range.

Looking for trouble. These Grumman fighters established an outstanding record against the Japanese.

faster and had better firepower and protective armor for the pilots.

The U.S. Navy's greatest combat record of the war was set on February 1, 1945, when Air Group 80 with Hellcats shot down 71 Japanese airplanes. This fantastic victory was achieved with the loss of only three Hellcats! On another occasion an F6F squadron attacked 40 Zeros and shot down 33 of them while losing only four planes.

Other data (F6F-5): Wing span, 42 feet 10 inches; length, 33 feet 7 inches; loaded weight, 12,730 pounds; engine, 2,100-horsepower Pratt & Whitney Double Wasp; maximum speed, 371 miles per hour at 20,000 feet.

His engine running at full power, a Hellcat pilot watches the deck officer for the signal to take off.

Above: **An F6F comes in for a carrier landing.** *Below:* **This pilot got two Zeros before his crash landing.**

GLOSTER METEOR

While it was the Germans who produced the world's first jet-propelled airplane, the first Allied warplane powered with the new engine was the British Gloster Meteor. It was also the only Allied jet to see active combat in the war.

The first experimental jet in England was the Gloster-Whittle, which was taken up for its maiden flight on May 15, 1941. While this test model was still being built, the British Air Ministry placed a contract for 12 Meteors. The first of these was taken into the air on March 5, 1943.

Squadron No. 616 became the first operational unit in the Royal Air Force to receive the new twin-jet fighters. The squadron had previously flown Spitfires, and its first seven Meteors arrived on July 12, 1944. Less than a month later—August 4—a Meteor scored its first victory by bringing down a German V-1 "buzz-bomb" south of London. The plane's four 20-millimeter cannon abruptly jammed when the pilot tried to fire at the V-1, and he destroyed the German pilotless flying bomb by tipping it over with his wing!

Meteors became the first Allied jets to go into service with the Allies on the European Continent

Three views of the beautiful Gloster Meteor, which was the only Allied jet-propelled warplane to see action during the war. It had a speed of 585 m.p.h.

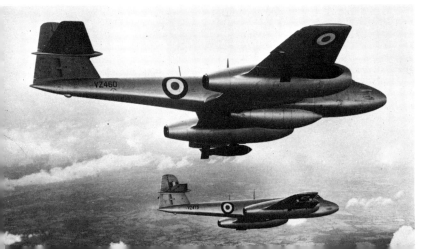

With his machine barely airborne, the pilot of this Meteor is already retracting his tricycle landing gear.

when part of Squadron No. 616 moved to Brussels, Belgium, in January, 1945. Most of their action was against troop concentrations and other ground targets, since by that time the German *Luftwaffe* had been almost completely destroyed.

Other data (Mark 4): Wing span, 37 feet 2 inches; length, 41 feet 4 inches; loaded weight, 15,175 pounds; engines, two 3,500-pounds-thrust Rolls-Royce Derwents; maximum speed, 585 miles per hour at sea level. (On November 7, 1945, a special Meteor set a world's speed record of 606.2 miles per hour, then raised the mark to 615.7 in 1946.)

OTHER HISTORIC PLANES OF WORLD WAR II

Above: The Curtiss SB2C Helldiver was the best U.S. Navy dive bomber. Below: Bell's P-39 Airacobra had its Allison engine in the fuselage behind the pilot.

Above: Last of the British biplane fighters, Gloster's trim Gladiators flew 253 m.p.h. Below: Douglas A-20 Havocs were used mostly for low-level work.

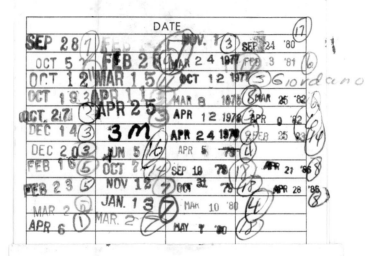